A Note to Parents

DK READERS is a compelling program for beginning readers, designed in conjunction with leading literacy experts, including Dr. Linda Gambrell, Director of the School of Education at Clemson University. Dr. Gambrell has served on the Board of Directors of the International Reading Association and as President of the National Reading Conference.

Beautiful illustrations and superb full-color photographs combine with engaging, easy-to-read stories to offer a fresh approach to each subject in the series. Each DK READER is guaranteed to capture a child's interest while developing his or her reading skills, general knowledge, and love of reading.

The five levels of DK READERS are aimed at different reading abilities, enabling you to choose the books that are exactly right for your child:

Pre-level 1: Learning to read
Level 1: Beginning to read
Level 2: Beginning to read alone
Level 3: Reading alone
Level 4: Proficient readers

The "normal" age at which a child begins to read can be anywhere from three to eight years old, so these levels are only a general guideline.

No matter which level you select, you can be sure that you are helping your child learn to read, then read to learn!

LONDON, NEW YORK, MUNICH,
MELBOURNE, and DELHI

Project Editor Esther Ripley
Art Editor Penny Lamprell
Senior Art Editor Clare Shedden
Series Editor Deborah Lock
US Editor Adrienne Betz
Production Shivani Pandey
Picture Researcher Marie Osborn
Jacket Designer Yumiko Tahata
Illustrator Peter Dennis
Indexer Lynn Bresler

Reading Consultant
Linda Gambrell, Ph.D.

Subject Consultant
Gillian Walnes
Anne Frank Educational Trust UK

First American Edition, 2001
12 13 15 14 13 12
Published in the United States by DK Publishing, Inc.
375 Hudson Street, New York, New York 10014
023-MB144P-May/2003

Published in Great Britain by Dorling Kindersley Limited

A Cataloging-in-Publication record is available
from the Library of Congress
ISBN-13: 978-0-7894-7380-6 (hb)
ISBN-13: 978-0-7894-7379-0 (pb)

Color reproduction by Colourscan, Singapore
Printed and bound in China by L Rex Printing Co., Ltd.

The publisher would like to thank the following for their
kind permission to reproduce their photographs.
t=top, b=below, c=center, l=left, r=right.
AFF/AFS Amsterdam the Netherlands: 4bl, 25tc, 30tc, 31br, 49br;
Juul Hondius 47tr. **Archive Photos:** 39br. **Corbis UK Ltd:**
Bettmann/Corbis 18bc, 22br, 37br; Hulton-Deutch Collection/Corbis
10br; Jacques M.Chenet/Corbis 42br; Michael John Kielty/Corbis
45tr; Todd Gipstein/Corbis 44tc. **Globe Trotter Network Sa
(France):** 45br. **Hulton Getty:** 15c, 34br. **Image Bank:** Anne Frank
Fonds, Basel/Anne Frank House, Amsterdam/Archive Photos 4tl,
9br, 9cr, 9tr, 11bl, 12ct, 30cr, 47br. **Swift Imagery, Swift Media:** 8tl.
Topham Picturepoint: 41bc. **Wiener Library:** 6bl, 19br.
All other images © Dorling Kindersley.
For further information see: www.dkimages.com

Discover more at
www.dk.com

Contents

 **READERS**

READING
3
ALONE

THE STORY OF
ANNE FRANK

Written by Brenda Ralph Lewis

DK Publishing, Inc.

Anne and her diary

Anne Frank age 12, in May, 1942

It was a warm summer's day, but the rain was pouring down, drenching the streets of Amsterdam. In spite of the heat, 13-year-old Anne Frank and her parents left home dressed in layers of clothing. Anne carried a satchel stuffed with things that she had gathered up in a hurry. The most precious was her new diary. Anne had already filled several pages with the events leading up to this day.

Anne Frank's precious diary

The date was July 6, 1942 – the day Anne's family had to go into hiding. They were hiding because they were Jewish, and Jews were being terrorized by the Nazi rulers of Germany. Now that the Nazis had occupied the Netherlands, the Franks were in great danger.

The Franks were afraid that they would be noticed on the long walk to their hiding place. They knew that the Nazis were rounding up Jews and sending them to camps. Most of them were never seen or heard of again.

The Franks' hiding place was an annex behind a warehouse where Anne's father had owned a business. The annex had a secret entrance and several rooms with blacked-out windows. From the outside, no one could tell that people were living there.

As Anne climbed the stairs to the annex, she was beginning a strange new life.

The hiding place was in this building.

For two years, she was not allowed to go outside and had to be quiet for most of the day. Anne described her life in her diary, but to know all about her story we have to go right back to the beginning.

The early years

Anne's first home in Marbachweg, Frankfurt

Anne Frank was born on June 12, 1929, in Germany in a city called Frankfurt. Her full name was Annelies, and she had a sister called Margot.

Margot (Mar-go) was three years older – a gentle, shy girl who was loved by everyone. Anne was full of life and was always asking questions. But no one could resist her sense of fun, least of all her father, Otto.

Otto Frank, Anne's father

Otto worked for a bank and lived with his wife, Edith, and his little girls in a comfortable apartment close to the countryside.

Edith Frank, Anne's mother

Until Anne was nearly four, she had a happy childhood full of good things. But then events in Germany changed the family's life forever.

Margot and Anne Frank

January, 1933
30

Adolf Hitler was the Führer, (Fure-er) or leader, of the Nazi Party. On January 30, 1933, he became ruler of Germany. Hitler blamed the Jews for many of the country's problems, and he began to make life difficult for them.

Jewish people began to lose their homes and their jobs, and the rest of the German people were told to have nothing to do with them. The Franks moved to another neighborhood where people were still friendly, but every day the situation was getting worse.

Adolf Hitler

Adolf Hitler was a dictator, which meant he had complete control of Germany. Huge crowds of Nazi followers gathered to listen to his speeches.

Horrible slogans about Jews were scrawled on the windows of Jewish-owned stores, and there were stories of punishments and beatings in the streets.

Otto Frank decided to move his family to Amsterdam in the Netherlands. He believed they would be safer there, among the Dutch people. And so they were – for a while.

Anne, nearest to the scooter,
playing with her friend, Sanne

Anne's new home, was an apartment on Merwedeplein (MER-vay-de-plain) in Amsterdam. She soon made new friends. Some of them were Jewish children whose families had also fled from Germany.

Anne and her friends liked to play hopscotch on the wide sidewalks and race along on their bicycles and scooters. Hide-and-seek and tag were favorite games on the grassy playground outside the Franks' apartment. In the winter, Anne loved to ice skate.

Anne grew into a happy, popular girl who loved to make people laugh. Sometimes she was in trouble at school for talking too much. One teacher gave her the nickname "Mistress Chatterbox."

Anne at school in Amsterdam

But when Anne was 10, her life was turned upside down all over again.

Dangerous times

May, 1940
10

The Germans were still very close, just across the border. In April, 1940, they conquered Norway and Denmark. Then on May 10, German troops began their invasion of Luxembourg, Belgium – and the Netherlands.

It was a Friday, but all the shops were closed, and Anne did not go to school. Every few minutes, she heard the wail of sirens warning of air raids.

German invasion
World War II began on September 3, 1939, when Germany invaded Poland. By 1940, Hitler had conquered much of Europe.

After four days of fighting, the Netherlands surrendered. Now the Dutch people, and the Jews who had fled from Germany, were under Nazi rule. Some Jews tried to sail to England, but German troops blocked the ports.

Trucks loaded with Nazi soldiers arriving in the main streets of Amsterdam

At first, life under Nazi occupation carried on as normal. The shops re-opened, and everyone had enough to eat. Anne and Margot went back to school, and their father went to work.

Otto Frank moved his business to a building on a street called Prinsengracht (PRIN-sen-hakt). Anne and her friends often played there, using the telephones and typewriters and daring each other to trickle water onto passers-by below.

Anne loved the movies and collected pictures of famous film stars. She also loved to swim at the local pool.

But, as time went on, the Nazis made more and more rules against the Jews. Anne found she was barred from most of her favorite activities and many places that she had been free to visit.

January, 1941 A new rule was introduced in January, 1941 – Jewish people were no longer allowed to go to the movies. They were also banned from going to the beach in the summer. Anne was very upset when swimming pools were also closed to Jews.

In September, Anne had to leave her school and go to a Jewish school instead.

Jewish families were terrified of breaking the new laws.

Everywhere – in libraries, theaters, museums, coffeehouses, and the zoo – signs were put up which said "Forbidden to Jews." Jewish people were forced to give up their bicycles and cars and were forbidden to use trams. Sometimes, Anne got a lift on a ferry from the ferrymen.

"It's not the fault of the Dutch that we Jews are having such a bad time," she wrote in her diary.

Then all Jews were ordered to wear yellow badges – a six-pointed Star of David, a Jewish symbol.

Yellow stars

The yellow star had the word "Jood" (Dutch for "Jew") picked out in black letters. The badge meant that Jewish people were to be treated as outcasts.

June, 1942
12

June 12, 1942, was Anne's thirteenth birthday. Despite the hard times, she got lots of presents. Otto gave her a red and light-green checked notebook with a metal lock. This was to be Anne's diary. The first thing she wrote was: "I hope you will be a great support and comfort to me."

By this time, life under Nazi rule had become almost unbearable, but Anne found that keeping her diary helped. She treated it as her friend and even gave it a name – "Kitty."

At first, she wrote about ordinary things – the hot weather, her exam results, and the boys she liked. But the entry Anne made on Sunday, July 5, 1942, was much more serious: "Father is talking about going into hiding."

The secret annex

At the end of June, the Germans announced that all Jews would soon be sent to work camps in Germany. Otto Frank told Anne that he would not allow his family to be "hauled away."

For months, Otto had been secretly preparing a family hiding place in an annex behind the offices and warehouse on Prinsengracht. Every week, he had been sending furniture, sheets and blankets, kitchen equipment, and food to the annex in a company van.

The SS

The SS were the Nazi political police. Their job was to track down Jews or anyone else who opposed the Nazis. People were terrified of them.

 July, 1942
5

Then, on July 5, there was terrible news. Margot received papers telling her to report to the SS – the Nazi political police – the very next day. She was only 16, but she and other young Jews were being sent away to Germany to one of the work camps.

Now the Frank family had to act fast. They decided that they would go into hiding in the annex the following day.

Margot went early the next morning, cycling through the streets with Miep Gies (Meep Hees), Otto's secretary. If they had been caught, both would have been punished severely.

Anne and her parents arrived soon afterward. Later, she described her new home – there were three bedrooms, a tiny washroom, a toilet, a large room with a stove and a sink, and an attic.

Anne's cat

Anne had to leave her cat to be cared for by neighbors. She wrote later: "Moortje, my cat, was the only living thing I said goodbye to."

Anne's favorite pictures on the wall of her room

Anne pasted up pictures of film-stars in the bedroom she shared with Margot to make it feel more like home. But it was going to be a very crowded home – four other people would soon be arriving to share their hiding place.

Life in hiding

On July 13, another Jewish family, Hermann and Auguste van Pels and their son Peter, came to stay in the secret annex. Four months later, Fritz Pfeffer, a dentist who was a friend of Anne's parents, also arrived. Now, eight people were hiding there.

During the day, when the workers were in the warehouse below, everyone had to speak in whispers. They did not dare to run water from the faucets or flush the toilet. If the floor creaked or they dropped something, someone might suspect that Jews were hiding there.

Living like this got on everyone's nerves. Anne wrote about the time Mr. and Mrs. van Pels argued so loudly she was sure that people would hear.

27

Several brave people took great risks to look after the hideaways and keep their secret. The SS were very hard on anyone found helping Jews.

Victor Kugler, the owner of the warehouse, had a false bookcase built to cover the entrance to the annex.

Miep Gies put herself in danger almost every day, trying to buy enough food for the families in hiding.

"She goes out every day in search of vegetables," Anne wrote, "and then cycles back with her purchases in large shopping bags." Miep used forged coupons to buy food, but luckily, the Nazis never caught her.

Bep Voskuijl (Vosh-kal), an office worker, smuggled milk into the annex and brought clothes for Margot and Anne when they outgrew their old ones.

Pages from Anne's diary, and her photo album

Living in hiding was very hard for Anne. After a year and a half in the annex, she wrote: "I long to ride a bike, dance, whistle, look at the world, feel young and know that I'm free, and yet I can't let it show."

It was difficult for such a lively girl to spend hours without talking or moving around, and Anne was often in trouble.

"Margot is naturally good and clever," she wrote, "but I seem to have enough mischief for the two of us."

At least Anne could tell her diary how she felt. She wrote that she loved her father best of all because he stood up for her when other people picked on her. Only the diary "knew" that Anne at first thought Peter van Pels was "lazy and stupid", but later she grew fond of him. Anne also described her hopes and dreams – how she longed to be a writer, to be grown up, and to fall in love.

Lessons in the annex
While they were in hiding, Anne and Margot learned languages, math, geography and history. They read many books and listened to the radio.

Captured by Nazis

The families in hiding were always afraid that they would be discovered. Any sound might mean danger.

One night in April, 1944, the men from the annex heard burglars breaking into the warehouse below and went down to investigate.

April, 1944

The thieves ran away, but two neighbors heard noises and also came to check. Now the men from the annex had to flee. They raced upstairs and pulled closed the bookcase door.

The bookcase door to the annex

Worst of all, the police turned up. They searched the building and arrived in the room that led to the annex.

Anne heard their footsteps in the room below. One of the policemen rattled the false bookcase that covered the doorway. Then he rattled it again.

Anne wrote: "A shiver went through everyone. I heard several sets of teeth chattering, no one said a word."

At last, the footsteps went away.

She added: "None of us has ever been in such danger as we were that night."

Outside, in Amsterdam, there were many enemies. The most dangerous were people who gossiped about Jews who were living in secret. The SS offered bribes to people who were prepared to give them information.

But after almost two years in hiding, Anne believed that the families in the annex would be rescued soon. On June 6, 1944, there was exciting news on the radio – Allied forces had landed on the coast of Normandy in northern France.

D-Day
June 6, 1944, was called D-Day. Thousands of British and US troops invaded Normandy to liberate northern France.

Anne told her diary: "... I have the feeling that friends are on the way."

But before the Allied troops could reach Amsterdam, all Anne's dreams of rescue were destroyed. On August 4, 1944, an informer telephoned the Gestapo, the Nazi secret police, and told them that Jews were hiding at 263 Prinsengracht. No one knows for sure who gave them away.

When the police arrived at the offices
in Prinsengracht, they knew exactly
where to look. They forced Victor
Kugler to open the bookcase door that
led to the secret annex.

The police gathered all the hideaways together at gunpoint and arrested them. Then they searched the annex for money and jewelry. They opened the old briefcase where Anne kept her diary, but found nothing there that interested them. The diary and loose pages were dumped out onto the floor.

The police marched their prisoners down the stairs and put them in a truck. When they had gone, Miep Gies put Anne's diary in a drawer to keep it safe until Anne came home again.

Anne's diary
By 1944, Anne's writing filled the diary her father had given her plus three notebooks, and a bundle of loose pages.

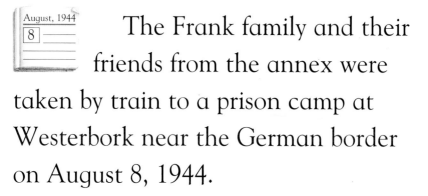

August, 1944
8

The Frank family and their friends from the annex were taken by train to a prison camp at Westerbork near the German border on August 8, 1944.

Anne and Margot and their parents had their hair cropped and had to wear prison clothes and wooden shoes.

They were put to work in a factory breaking up old batteries. It was hard, dirty work, but, after more than two years of being indoors, Anne could at least feel the sun on her face sometimes.

But three weeks later, the family was sent to Auschwitz-Birkenau (Aowsh-vitz Burk-en-aow) – a concentration camp set up by the Nazis to get rid of people they considered to be "undesirable." Hundreds of thousands of people were put to death there. The Franks were in the very last train load of people to be sent from the Netherlands to this terrible camp.

Families on the journey to Auschwitz

 Anne and Margot were in Auschwitz for only a few weeks. Then the two girls were sent on alone to another camp called Bergen-Belsen – it was also a terrible place, full of dirt and disease.

The prisoners there had so little food that they were starving. It was winter, and Anne and Margot had nothing but rags to wear. Freezing and hungry, they caught a deadly fever called typhus, and, some time in February or March, 1945, Margot died. Anne had lost her sister and felt sure that her father and mother must have died in Auschwitz. She was desperately ill herself, and died a few days after Margot.

But one member of the Frank family had survived. In January, 1945, Allied Russian soldiers advanced into Poland. When they reached Auschwitz, they set free the prisoners who had survived.

Anne's mother had died just a few weeks before the camp was liberated, but Otto Frank was still alive.

Russian soldiers freeing prisoners from Auschwitz

Telling Anne's story

 On May 7, 1945, Germany surrendered and World War II came to an end. The world was at peace again after nearly six years of fighting. Otto Frank returned to Amsterdam to look for Anne and Margot.

It was difficult to find out what had happened to people who had been sent to camps, but in July, Otto learned that both of his daughters were dead. In fact, everyone else from the annex had died. Only Otto had survived.

Miep Gies

Miep Gies is now in her nineties and still lives in Amsterdam. She has been given many honors for the kindness she showed to the families in the annex.

But not everything had been destroyed or lost. Miep Gies still had Anne's diary. She had hoped to return it to Anne, but now she gave it to Otto.

Otto read Anne's diary over and over again. Eventually, he decided that everyone should be able to read her story of their life in hiding.

Covers of all the different editions of Anne's book

Otto turned Anne's diary into a book, which was published in the Netherlands in 1947. It was translated into many other languages and was published in the United States in 1952 as *Anne Frank: The Diary of a Young Girl.*

Now, more than 25 million copies of Anne's book have been sold. The girl who had dreamed about becoming a writer is now one of the most famous authors in the world, and plays and films have been made about her life.

Many countries have memorials to Anne Frank. When people think of Anne, they think of her courage, her sense of humor, and her hopes for the future. They also remember the many other people whose lives have been destroyed by prejudice and war.

A statue of Anne Frank in Utrecht

An animated film
One of the most recent versions of Anne's story is a French animated film called *Anne Frank's Diary.*

The front offices at 263 Prinsengracht today

The secret annex behind the warehouse and offices at 263 Prinsengracht is still there today. The rooms were emptied long ago, but in 1960, they were opened as a museum called The Anne Frank House. Every year, hundreds of thousands of visitors from all over the world, climb the stairs behind the bookcase door. They walk through the rooms where the Frank family and their friends lived and try to imagine what it was like to be in hiding there for more than two years.

Children reading Anne's diary in the museum

Anne's favorite pictures are still pasted on the wall, and a few personal belongings of the people in hiding are on display.

Even though terrible things had happened to Anne and her family, she was sure that people could make the world a better place. "In spite of everything," Anne wrote in her diary, "I still believe that people are really good at heart."

Anne Frank
1929-1944

Glossary

Allied troops/Allies
The joint forces of Britain, France, the USA, Russia, and others fighting against Germany in World War II.

Annex
Rooms that are an extension to a main building.

Border
The line where two countries meet.

Bribe
A promise of money or a favor to encourage a person to do something.

Concentration camps
Death camps set up by the Nazis in Germany and occupied countries. Millions of Jews and other groups of people were imprisoned and killed.

Coupons
Tickets issued to a person to buy fixed amounts (rations) of food in wartime.

D-Day
June 6, 1944, the day the Allied forces landed in France and began the liberation of Europe.

Diary
A book used to record a person's private thoughts about everyday and important events.

Ferry
A boat for transporting passengers.

Gestapo
The secret state police in Nazi Germany.

Invasion
Taking control of a foreign country by military force.

Jews
People who follow a religion called Judaism. Christianity and Islam developed from Judaism. The ancient Hebrew people in the Bible are considered to be the ancestors of modern Jews.

Liberation
Setting people or a country free.

Nazi
A member of the National Socialist German Workers' Party, which took control of Germany in 1933.

Occupation
Holding on to power in a foreign country.

Outcast
A person who is excluded from the rest of a community.

Prejudice
Dislike of an individual or a group of people based on ideas that are false.

Typhus
A deadly disease carried by lice.

World War II
A war that lasted from 1939 to 1945. Allied forces on one side fought against Germany, Japan, and Italy on the other side.